Daylily

Called It

a Dangerous

Moment

Daylily

Called It

a Dangerous

Moment

ALESSANDRA LYNCH

ALICE JAMES BOOKS
FARMINGTON, MAINE

10 9 8 7 6 5 4 3 2 1

Alice James Books are published by Alice James Poetry Cooperative, Inc.,
an affiliate of the University of Maine at Farmington.

Alice James Books
114 Prescott Street
Farmington, ME 04938
www.alicejamesbooks.org

Library of Congress Cataloging-in-Publication Data

Names: Lynch, Alessandra, 1965- author.
Title: Daylily called it a dangerous moment / by Alessandra Lynch.
Description: Farmington, ME : Alice James Books, [2017]
Identifiers: LCCN 2016046101 (print) | LCCN 2016054521 (ebook) | ISBN
   9781938584657 (paperback : alk. paper) | ISBN 9781938584701 (eBook)
Subjects: | BISAC: POETRY / American / General.
Classification: LCC PS3612.Y54 A6 2017 (print) | LCC PS3612.Y54 (ebook) | DDC
   811/.6--dc23
LC record available at https://lccn.loc.gov/2016046101

Alice James Books gratefully acknowledges support from individual donors, private foundations,
the University of Maine at Farmington, the National Endowment for the Arts, and the Amazon
Literary Partnership.

Cover art: "Time" by Metka Krašovec, Acrylic tempera on canvas, 81x100 cm, 1992.

Contents

For the survivors

Snail, snail, glister me forward,
Bird, soft-sigh me home,
Worm, be with me.
This is my hard time.

Theodore Roethke

First air and light suffuse us—
daylily, oriole, dust—
then love, that airborne thing.
We become forgetful, leave doors and windows
open—the room adrift
with pollen-druff, beetle-husk—
the world's quick dispatch signifying
the end, and more gorgeous telegrams await—
pin oak leaf, darkening canal, little horses fenced
by highway, clouds, your face.
     The dead bits fighting in the wind drift in.

What more to wrestle? What else to woo?
Close, door. Close, petal. Human eye, you close too.

I.

Excavation

excavation: the bone that has no marrow

Let it dry—let it dry in the ditch—
a roadside bone—innocuous.
Still, hard to reckon with.

> You don't know the who of it, barely the what
> but once it belonged & longed & had stride. Now it rises from the
>   poke
> & takes your hand as though for a walk

through rain & it is alive again, a man, urging you on
to mr. anonymous
who coaxes & spends you & swings you by another name. Who never
    gives his own.

> How bloodless he is. Sitting at the white table. Handsome shirt.
And below: tight pants filled with nothing. Undercover matador.
More bloodless than this bone you've found.
> Ask no more about bone. Don't breathe or swallow.
The stinging
belt, your buckled hip, the blade
> chucking your chin, drawn down your neck,
> angling toward the breast.

Don't ask about the voice that snarled and nested in your ear.
You lived in hoax and hoax is fog. No charm of finches to blast it clear.
His charm: all harm—

                                        and names?

His / yours. Don't ask.

excavation deux

some perversion of a travolta movie
where the girl is swerving in her spotlight and the guy heats up and woos her
from spotlight to parking lot mercury light and woos her from the strobe to his
throb-throb and / cut to black / but there is no flame or steam between them
only she a stifled scream a horse arrears and he a knife pressed into her flank
and thigh into her human pelvis the knife screwing in as though to fix a wall or
make a shelf. He makes her a wall and shelves her then.

would have lowered

Your body   ribboned
by strobe   your hips   fluidly blue
in the shafts   face quartered by light   wrists slashed
by the green threads of it   shoulder bronzed

in the glow of disregard   half-
lidded eye   perfect interior repose
your pelvis tilting   dipping its axis
in all that gloss   gloss in all that

flat light of his knife   The window
dropping its blinds   Your body
felled swiftly   from its dance

I could have taken your hand   I could have led you
like a moonlit horse   beyond shadowy bars
beyond paddock   beyond what had harnessed you   what had
wrenched your jaw   lamed your tongue

I would have lowered you
to earth   beyond myrtle   rhododendron   cyclamen
I would have lowered you there
away from the light that dismantled you

berries

Berries breed and brood and darken
in scarlet dusk. Their viscera
visible. Their contortions
evident. A smear on the pave.
A tiny massacre.
Seed-eyes dull with sun won't meet yours.
You who had stepped over them
proclaiming *it's the order of things.*

no pronouncements

On a small hill grew a bullhorn rose.
It was making no pronouncements.

———

Beyond the hooded moon, the stars would not
unleash their light. My fingers
cold with summer could not button
my shirt. The fingers had been
imperiled. Jinxed.

———

No curtains hung
between where it happened and hadn't. The man
I worked with looked at me,
shrewd. He'd seen
my dull face. His neck veins
tightened. He flipped
something grill-wise, said
I'll kill him.

———

The absent-me wrung out
a rag, turning away from the sink,
away from the wall, flat
as a hand pressed over a mouth.

—It was air that had forced me down,
pinned me, heaved till I
became little of a self

    with a little thought:

Check for blood regardless.

———

Flat in parking lot dirt I turned
for orientation, eye to eye
with something glinty—rim misshapen,
half-sunk metal. I could be
alive

only to flowers and birds,
the stricken
fields and fields and fields of them.

The human?
(could he be a he—a being—what he
did—undid—
what could be only
un-being)

Like air: memory
Memory: like air
I walk through and
disappear

It hangs and hangs and hangs—
not bell, not noose.

A case of walking paralysis.
A case of can't-report.

Glance
at the shack, the tree. Nothing
looks back.

Knife-I-am-ready-
to-pull, are you ready
to gleam

in the lot
where I could not
scream?

Shock me past
the blacking out.
Shock me awake—

speak for the mouth-that-was-mine,
for the voice, triple-strapped
in its jacket, marching on.

wake

after sinking into gin   morning drops a gentle rain
encasing the unseen   *unmentionable*   clouds enfold
wasps-in-a-shroud   stay aloft   without a string
unmentionable   even after headstrong long-gone spins of wind

(go go little gallop of smoke   lithe cantering steam
come come wild unthreadings   anything not
to envision his fingers pressed against the orchid's
throat   his intentional ramming)

limp river: a dance

limp river she was   stretched   among men
& their bend   their garbled hands   stretched her
from stone to stone   ribboned her around
the heron's leg   propped her
head on a stabbing rock
thrust fistfuls of minnows through her veins
          & when they wrung her flesh
to drips   the bank bled
the deer stood around
in stiff registry
the audience clapped

the club

was really a shack.
In four steps, you could back out into the lot
and its smoky light. In two steps, cut

through the mechanical whir
of the strobe. The slam-slam hiss.
Ice thinning in its glass.

One squat toilet in the stall—
yellowmouthed—under light too dim
for you to discern blood from dirt.

You were there to lose yourself. There
from loneliness, for love of dancing. You said
you felt safe in the center

of the strobe, a manic flower,
petals whirling so fast
they could disintegrate.

They always played your song, and when you
climbed the steps to the DJ in his corner, how tiny he was
behind bulletproof glass, turning

knobs, adjusting the bass. Dull beat-boom-thud.
You tapped, said *I'm sorry* and looked out at the floor,
unwieldy with humans.

Before you made your request, the DJ began
crying: *Are you clean, are you clean? Nobody's clean—all my friends*
in the pit, needles and smoke, all my friends gone

dirty, all gone. You're not clean.
Can't be. Still you stared at his face, asked for Prince,
and returned the next night—severed

purple and gold and green by the strobe—
intent on dancing hard
till the man got littler, littler till

the club-light fizzles, till there is only the outside
air that will not rise above
zero.

the outside air

Though it's still blue, the mist here is not the future mist and the rain not the same rain and the corner field not a parking lot. No sound from the pond. No after-stir. Charred flies skitter over its silent vellum, and chimney swifts dodge the irrefutable air. And there are other alterations, other speeds.

From underfoot, doves startle. Leaves hang their dry masks over the trail, rattling slightly. On the western bank, a tree—aloof from its cutoff dress—all sheathed bark, reads as skin, reads as: can-be-shed. Will-be-pared.

The air once deep enough to breathe, too shallow to wade. Broken-armed women sinking and rising. Their mouths, fixed as megaphones. Their faces undone.

pond & flies

the flies greeded for eye-light   wanted at it
swarmed to the wet target   heard what was dead
in there   what had been   occluded
what had narrowed the focus

        at first they edged
and frayed it   their wiry legs couldn't nudge
the eye back to sight   no   they wanted the dead of it
the soft meat of its tug   wanted
to end its end   the nth of it   wanted to feed
and fatten on what wouldn't start again

II.

Admission

1.
In the bleeding berries   on the nettle-hill
where pond was a ruse for calm
I gave voice
to what deadened the field   what ended its green
said the word *assault*, prettier than *r*____.

Violets whitened.
The thing shrank from its essence.

The word took breath to say   this pushing air away
(*dislodge it from the skin dislodge his breath from your face his voice*)

breath lost in one swift pull of winter.

After I said what I said   said the word
assault was prettier. Assault was less
invasive. R____ would mean admission and surrender.

The words took breath.
(*Hush, hush. Come, forgiveness.*)

2.

It took seconds for him
to push me down then he was done—

I was supine. Perpendicular, the tree. That night
we made a kind of staggering diagram in the parking lot.
How had he risen from me? Jerked out, rolled
off.

       Crude knuckles scuffed by fatigue and dust, the roots
of the tree inches from my face. Had he gripped
my wrist, pressed a knife at my neck?

For decades I've walked in a daze
      through insect-amputees who are not dead
but don't have the gut or grip to shield their good
remaining legs. They're scuttle-dry and yellow-gray
      as storm-gripped sky.
For decades I've walked
      in a daze through this day's recitations.
Low crawl of red through leaves.

I pulled myself up. Parallel, the tree. That night
we made a kind of shuddering frame for the air.
How had he gotten me down? Had he seized
      my arm or waist…I don't remember the least.

III.

In Another Country

adios

Who mothered her? Silence and glass.
Who fathered her? The phoebe's haunt.
What sustains her? The rain.
—What rushes off,
returns as steam, soft things,
the slinking *adios*. The mind wills her
to disappear, wisp beyond
flyspeck and seed, to live
as aftersmoke—the eke
of light in the marrow. What keeps
her here? Barely. By a hair.

wolf

The father kept aloof till he heard the faint howl
and glimpsed his daughter shudder and drop.
Did he need to open her shirt to examine the bruise
while she strained away.
Did he need to know how deeply the teeth
sank, if a pack had tracked mud through
her blood. Was he checking to see whether they left
scars on her skin,
that wore his mark first, that belonged to him.

mothers said:

van means evanescence   means the planet will
evaporate   his cruddy hand will
yank you in   he will tie you with his yo-yo
string   pack your mouth with magazines

his eyes blank tenements   or bottle caps
gas-scum skin   slit grin   pink
rattling dashboard chains   mothers said: look
around   every bend   every swing of road
for a blue van   black van   what's windowless   scare fast

from the sky sulphuring itself   he won't refuse
his impulse   but make refuse of your flowers
incinerating rainbow lunchpails
little shoes   dirty lace   patent-scuff
ditched like black tires   approximately size 6
bloom-rot won't vanish   mothers said
quickly dropping their faces

panties

They are girly   frillishly dizzy   splattered
pink or dark   sequin twist of scarlet
riotous yellow   crumpled bloom   bow-ridden & festooned
or plain as a napkin for one polite cough
They are printed *hot-stuff* or *come-and-get-it*
lacily feathered   given to flight   or stickered with princess
& swing set or broody red lip-print & tongue-lick
leopard-hide   zebra-skin   a satin slide-down quickie
How many eye-lets   How much crotch   banded or not

They are bandage or wing when you wear them
& when men yank them   they sink like a limp
flag   meaty breath across your face   dead animal
breath that can not resuscitate
even while he and he and he heave & you go absent
below   panties crudding with the blood
the dry flies crave   You do not
bury them   You do not fold
launder or throw them away
into a public receptacle but leave them
where they lie: small as a child's   too scared
to stir a stitch   to snitch
a little wilt around your ankles

blows & burns

she's dragging the doll by its flopping arm
its lank hanks   in her high heels   dragging the doll
down the bannister   by the wrought-iron grate   propping her
in the crotch of a tree   where the doll sags a little
she's heaving the doll over her back   or by the wrist
dragging the doll into the garden   burying her head
in the bee-swarmed roses   the faltering petals   she's making
a thorny crown   dressing her in two different faces   dragging
the doll into pews   dropping her on benches   she is
shooting her with light   every stitch has her attention   dragging
the wigged doll   she wearing a wig as well   neither one speaking
only she jaggedly breathing and dragging   the doll
around   setting her up for the flash   for the swift shoot
the taking

gang bang

was the village against us
we didn't beg   stoppered
by all four corners of the field   bed   pool table   yard
didn't beg beautifully   didn't splay-leg
didn't play dead   already were
gang bang was the village
disillusioning us   undoing our threads   revoking our knots
refuting us while feeling us up   fueling and refueling
its dead engines   flooding gas into our mouth
to get it to start

les demoiselles d'avignon

The one we look at as the one cursed
and framed
hangs her orange beast-face, a block for a breast

angular, vacant might-be eyes or maybe some shape
screwed to fit the composition of the idea, the abstraction,
the thing,
a smile or simply a slit through which you can draw
your ticket and enter the gate
(I'm afraid, sir, you'll find only paint)

...he was using the vague semblance of women
to turn the century

crude nudes, meat too pink, too undercooked
to eat or flay or were they pre-flayed, tenderized
women dressing their hair, corkscrewed eyes
in the mirror, part-skin, part-stone
oh, but look at those tones!

—fit for the tomb—
a box with limited shadow
so there was limited light
around them

frida says (a translation)

i will cut off all my hair and use each strand
as another bar of music   each bird an unbridled note

i want the dark birds   they're more easily read
they can use my hair as nesting threads

you have said you won't love me without
my woman power—what protects—my veil

i say: my burden—what strangles—dead tendrils
of pleasing   pleasing   appeasing

follicles which have no sheen or motion
i sit on my hellish yellow chair without my hair shirt

in my man's suit and small man's shoes   my legs wide
like a man's   smoke issuing from fingers

immaterial   green bird in my lap

hardhats

Those orange hardhats
Those orange witching cones
and the sun flaying her neck where the road splits
like the pried-open legs
of language. She walks between

men, between sandbags and shovels, shoves and hoots.
Somebody catcalls, someone cajoles. What else
to do but be a vanished thing?—

    drop into the pothole he's filling
    w/ tar and semen, pave the skin, become a sector of the road

(burlap-slump, pebble eyes)
the blurred meridian we rush by.

in another country

in another country the women are fed and fed by their men till dull
their bellies dragging from room to room
unceasingly fed lest they burn a little off   lest they thin out
their perfect skin obscene as the moon-beyond-full lopsided wheezing
    what are they doing growing enormous losing their chins
      mouths
    swallowed by their own flesh then eyes then nose then
    can't smell his approach again

clit

Someone got her clit cut
Someone blindered her
led her into the pit
to keep her clit unlit
Keep it clipped
shut
slit
No pleasure now
No meow
Keep it a spit in the dark   keep it dark
Keep it safe   stuffed   keep it so it had enough
Keep it writ
unwrit
Sit without it
Tie back the lobe
Dog screel keen
Keep her on the mark   make her the mark
marketable
Make her market
Table her
Mongrel who done her in
Mongrel
and a twisted yellow rag mongering of it
What a butterfly   what a lie   to dare
write about her as though she is
a flower

small door in the fog

My sister says *why*
forgiveness which I think of as a small door in the fog
that I might slip through,

hauling the women—
their blown glass, their smithereens—
in a little sack—

that we might un-body:

not drop them,
not set them
to flight.

That I might hold us,
our silence

unremarkable in my hands
that won't stop quivering, no matter what.

IV.

Foretell the Silent Ridge
of the Tongue

I lose the street to the street to the street,
circling beneath blue sobs of night-
clouds, the moon dryly distant. A framework
of trees, the only boundary to my weaving.
I drag one branch that has lost
its trunk, leaving a leafy wake. It has little heft, a light collar,
a thin wrist, and I drag it while circling,
nearly convincing myself recursiveness
is flight and I am skyward-bent.

When the yellow bird dropped
from the tree, I did not think
to name it. Its beak clacked, its thin tongue
flickered. The gray eye was like
the lidded human eye of someone
I had loved far back. The wings
beat against dirt. I did not cover it
with a leaf or prod it to stop but continued
to watch its failing heart.
After it died, I did not touch
its yellow precision but drew a careful circle
to mark its compass points—tail-feathers
fanned out, head oddly twisted,
legs gnarled as twigs—to mark
its transformation, to mark my witness.

Ward off bangs & blows, quiet the grass in its ransacked field.
Seek hard things to keep the body safe. Seek stone.
If stone's a murderous clank, circle the pitted world. Quiet
the owl in its damaged wood. Feign being air—maneuver
between star & dirt. Reel hard from your wound. Err as bang
& blow, find safety in the wind. Flick on snow for light. Sit still
with falling things & soft bits like rain.

Fox in the woods today, an emblem
of female. Bee flew past a puddle—
in her wake, doves shot
between branches. I kept
glimpsing my sisters—
bluestar with curtailed stem, mouth
of pond unraveling, cattails
in wild corners.
  This was my only weather—
following the unseen, sniffing for evidence
that it had been.

When the body revoked itself
and slimmed to bone and light, it became
the very mouth of longing and so no longer
longed. It drifted through circumscribed
worlds without hunting, only haunting. It was
beautiful this way—like trees in rain,
or a train in snow, moving motionless,
the voice of voicelessness. It could have
lived forever, gliding, a circuitry
of light, flecked and sparking,
wiring the world it had abandoned.

Maybe it wasn't a him.
     Maybe it was a shadow from puppet-strings of light
     and smoke or a blindered horse bolting.
                    Maybe it was a bad-eyed animal
that limped and slurred. Maybe it was something that breathed but had
no shape.
Not him but a whack of dust.

———

Imagine being air that cannot drop
cannot land   cannot hurt

Imagine not being able to die
not having a hand in things

———

(Memory is a small patch of dirt
by a tree where nothing grows. An actual place.
The tree dead in its tracks.)

Give me your hand. May it turn from rope to flesh.
Where might I take you
        this time   only the facts   back
to the tree where you felled me
      where the tree did nothing but sprawl in moonlight
      O beautiful!
             (O tree!)

The way to steady what unsteadied me
was transformation:
gash to star, wound to window.

The way to make things stay was say goodbye:
farewell, dirging bell—go to flower! Farewell, oriole—
go to orange dust!

—his mask-face
dissolving until there was only
thought, that blank.

Chance—

with one hand you cradle
a lilac bundle, with the other
crush a human body.
     Both smell like rain

and the wheels of an anonymous train
hurtling through its tunnel
     carrying my unspeaking sisters.

I was flat as pool water while the hungry
rain slashed down. Was I more amorous
for memory's electric-blue static than for the actual?
Did I prefer the transparent flicking
against my skin to solid flesh? And danger—
was that my primary lover? How it turned
me hip-wise, swiveling my waist, singing
close and dirty in my ear.

I tear the questions into little squares
and heap them on a book
I won't be reading for a while.
They breathe half breaths, a small rustling
in the mouth, the susurrus preceding death.
A few flutter, but they mostly cling
to tattered siblings, quarantined from what
might signify. There is no other
way for me to mourn than having a hand
in things, tearing what is torn, keeping
vigil on the futile, unintelligible. Listen
closely to their frayed voices,
their dismembered music.

I beg to turn back
into smoke, steam, air,
back to what I was
when I hadn't known
the test and taste of flesh,
before I desired its blood, when
I was enamored only of heron and rain.
Desirous of nothing. Nil.
When the wind was my sister.

Can thinking wend a way
to where the body
feels? To where it quivers, retracts,

roots? Mind discontinues its thoughts. Dream dis-
continues the world. Light discontinues

day. A hammer. A bird
skull. Yesterday's hand covers
its mouth.

Something dead floats
down the street of bones—something insistently
alive arises from aftermath.

V.

P.S. Assault

1.
The girl it happens to
crawls out

of my body
straight into the grass that borders the lot
where she lies face up, a cloth
doll termites drill into, leaving tiny holes
   in her yellow cheek, the two heaps of her eyes,
   her flopping elbows—
where the once-mouth was:
leaves and wet dark.

I am sweeping up seed-husks and twigs
to clear a circle around her.
   I keep a respectable distance
while admiring how silent she is, how substantial,
how weightless.

   Something beautiful about her as she
perforates, eaten by mites and rot, something coolly autonomous
as though she never belonged to the body.

   Look again and the doll isn't a doll at all
but a lump in the grass, doubled over, small, hard-eyed as bone.

No assailant in view.

2.

Rape felt stripped. And spare. Brute.

   The daughters march with their blindfolds on,

   their dresses stiff-whipping around their bare ankles,

straight into the Arctic.

They make a voiceless parade,

   bleached as drift-sticks.

They move with the inevitability

of dreams. I am someone's daughter among them.

   *Once upon in a parking lot…*I said

repeatedly…then my voice faltered, fell off, my eyes distracted

by wind insistently pulling the curtains

apart and the dead flower in its glass of water.

3.

In the aftermath   she was a crude
figure: 2 stick-arms 2 stick-legs   streak
of blood   blurry crotch   no eyes
        no mouth—

legs repositioned   hair maladjusted
head propped   she his prop   or was she
        faint as starlight at the edge of dawn   faint
as a fawn's flank   spattered with so much universe

        she diminished—
human   hungry
for nothing.

4.

Shame is her orientation.

See the straight pink pines by the wildflower field, the black
eyes edged by petals staring through her? And the panic
of wild turkeys wherever she looms.

There are mosses and twigs and camouflage-rods in the forest,
and leaves in the dusty trees to hide behind.

But she awakens again, too clear, in that
memory…what she didn't do, what was done. The
cock-limp and stutter and smear—.

If I could slip you off—quick as cornsilk….
If you hadn't become my skin, Shame
If you hadn't become my shame, Skin

5.

dream-bee burst through an orange bloom
dream-bee burst through a bloomy world
dream-bee burst a blurry sea

burst me from the dream
o bee

the stranger heaved his weight on me
the stranger bore a hole in me
the stranger tore the me from me

leaden as the bullets
I keep on my sill
I am heavy and multiple

little helmets
        little tombs
        little pills

can't find the body that belongs to my voice
        or my voice that belongs to the harm

6.
the things she spat out:
glass bits and sour mash
    and she-was-fucked-to-a-blank-it-wasn't-her-doing

was it?

7.

Thinking in my thinking I'm making it alive flinching from my bloated
white shadow the lamp in the window is a man's hat the man waits in
the narrows to get me think it through hasn't he already gotten me or
this time I want to really feel it know it is me being pushed down close
to those exposed roots it is me think myself into staying embodied I
don't want to shudder apart like ash between December trees or drift
up like mindsmoke want to own up to my body I want to know it is my
body pressed into the cold ground by a stranger who had no second
thought no first or did he think I was a shimmer a hole an outlet an
animal was I his father or mother or did he see I had my own shape
shuddering as bodies do when they are sick with a virus I had a name
he didn't ask for oh now I'm thinking again he called me "Stephanie" as
though I would answer to that as though I were in his movie as though
we'd done things together he wasn't an animal after all he was human
and he wasn't and I was a thread so wavery so frayed nothing followed

8.
      you have to be a god to get away with it
and then the women always turning
into something else: bull-flower, frog, that laurel tree she asked to be

      I don't need a god to tell me to turn into a fox

I'm expert at the swift-lope-through-scarred-hills

9.

That girl who is me now? She's split apart.

    Like a starfish. Like mercury. You can find her alive

        in a small house by a dried-up sea. For decades she's been

            hoarding

        beach plums and stones....

Bring her bread, but no flowers—flowers signify

something alive, something that thrives even in sand.

    She smells of salt and blood. She won't ever

meet your eyes. Her skin is dust-dry.

If you pour water straight from the pitcher

down her throat, she won't flinch or grab

a rag when it splashes to the floor. She'll sit

slack in her straight-backed chair.

    Don't touch her hands—she'll tighten

her grip till you both turn white and cold, your lips

the greenish purple of unripe plums.

        Don't offer her a scarf—she'll knot it

        around your neck. Sand-flies will swarm

        from the linoleum, thicken around your shoulders,

      and she'll look straight through you as though you were

        the sea—

she'll begin to tell her story, the one with no beginning or ending.

    She'll recite it by heart—

10.

  Tracing it back can be helpful the doctor said Eons ago
this paper was stripped
from some tree in a boggy forest,
then wrenched through machines
  "the degree to which I was…"
falters in my throat.

  Now the package I ordered
arrives, and I am circling and eyeing it
as though it's critical—every surprise suspect—but there's nothing
beating inside this brown parcel and its
triply-knotted strings. Not meant
  to be opened.

Even things with no resemblance
to my assailant make me start—the gleaming nail in the door
is his unseeing eye fixed on me.
  Think it through she said *bring the moment back to present-thought*

The flowers clinging
to the electrocutionary fence around a jailyard
have mustard breath. Now they've vanished. I don't
remember his breath, or any sounds from his throat
as he thrust—did he really exist…? I am afraid
to open. Afraid he hurt someone else,
  I not having reported.

This package is nothing I want. A case
within an encasement, what it always is.

You have to retrain your brain she said
The brown paper around it fluttering and
drying and fluttering, the package unopened,
    trapped in its unruly twine.

The letters a blur I'm too tired to decipher.

Whatever I ordered is strapped in, unheaving, a weight
in this room.
    Hold it to the minute, don't cut it open, don't fling
the wrapping about, hold it to the minute…

    Rewrite the narrative she said

Rewrite she

VI.

Things

Things, things.
Limbs just limbs.

Why not live
within the world?

I was raped here. Don't
you think it time

I reappear?

Maybe I'd like to be found
in a flood, in an unwashed

gulley, in blood. Maybe
I'm afraid of being loved.

My body thinks
of infinite freedom—

a kiss that is
a kiss.

VII.

Daylily

When you entered the room in your dark
mask, you could have been the night. And when
you cupped the candle, your skin
flamed to a sable petal. And when you
opened the bed, opened the sheet,
you were opening a book—that much
tenderness.

    And then the dark mask bled
into an owl's, then an evening lake, then
a human face.

I fell into the world of your mouth—
the sky blacked out with desire,
a string of phoebes in high air suspended
two notes—
fleck of oriole, rushed flame.

Desire assaulted the trees,
     pushed stones into stones.

The sky was at a standstill.
     It sparked no cartwheel, shrugged off

directionals. The weather vane was a no-how
     wire. The clock revoked its dial. Desire
bred shadows in my throat—filled bags with dirt then emptied them,

     and when a slight breeze
blew through the skin, the longing flared again—

                    responsible villagers fled.

Woke early—a warm & gold stillness
asleep in the bed,
      a leopard, a dream
                        of death.
      I left my own body—gliding out
      to the pond to test how long
                    I could be gone before you'd vanish—
    a little weaving in the air, the stir of a twig
                enshadowed. Then I felt
the pierce of an arrow, or was it rain.

At the corners and edges of that space
we'd been wordless for, I willed your body
all morning—waiting for your shape
to cross the field, for emerald to go gold—
—stagger to glide. Waiting
at the interstice between desire
and loss.
      It was not until the body
floated off, incandescent, weak with want,
that I thought to move towards it.

                  a single flower   a strange bouquet
                  you mouthed the whole
                  bloom   had at
                  the root   pulled   till the bell .
                  dropped   in soft heaps

                  whispered at my neck
                  take   *take*

Once I had been inexorable, cold
toward the stars blossoming
inside me, little asterisks of being.
      Then my hood undid
its string. Time stepped
away, my body dissolved, and the stars broke out—

I could almost keep wanting you. For you
have an animal eye—part owl, part lynx. A bad eye,
too, half-covered by your hat, eye
on the wrong side of wild—. And your quiet
is too loud. How to fix that?

                              Pour buckets of tar,
smear polish from tins. Black out
the lack,

                              feed the night that holds
us, microscopic
glints—.

The day began in rope and furl.
The bandaged birch, black wire snaking
a wall. Ended with stone. You said
stone heavily. There was no other way
to say it. You said *stone* deliberately.
It must have been glacial,
a dark deposit—dead serious. Not
to be budged—exempt from the axe—.

It would take eons of wind to pry you
loose. I said *what about
the pebble and crystalline sand? What about
mutability?* The night stood
transparent. And rain, my wavering
companion, shimmered,
and when I lay my hand upon
your stone, it glistened.

Something wrong. The alphabet
frozen in its theater. You disappeared,

returned with tiny pliers, a glittering screw,
and removed the blue hood

of the typewriter, jostled the keys. You removed
a few tight springs, a latch, a thin ring, your hands

darkening with ink as you worked, unasked,
unsummoned, while I watched the bits

of my world—jangling, disoriented,
mouthing tinselly syllables—pile up
around you.

Flying on ether and velvet, nothing
      to fetter them, no planetary manacles—.
The Perseids loved, as we did, the high
dead branches of sycamore and elm.
      They were brilliant minutes
            blistering down, ardent suicides, streaking
            to earth, which would receive their gleams,
                          cool their fevers
                                    as they sputtered out.

Memory took off its hat,
set down its cane, melted
into the undone side of the bed.

    No room for me in that house—
too many birds, too few ideas.

    The yard's frothy-mouthed forsythia
I needed to gag. No air in the color blue, no air.

    Autumn's strewn bodies instructive
and beautiful but hard to look at.

    Maybe I needed focus. *Pull
the cord tight, loosen the wire. Let the bells
tell it right.*

    There was the hole in the wall, my hurt
fist, my frantic plastering.

    Something else staggering through the door.

It was an impossible house
with difficult doors. Halls veered
through empty. Even the semblance
of the self was lost, even the mothering
of self and of semblance—lost.

    There were stirrings in the next room. At first
I thought *death*—low burr, rustle,
a hopeful noise—. No,

                               it was the amalgam of emptiness,
piles of light on the sill, amber dust sifting
through. The nothing of the thing.

Daylily called it a dangerous moment. It teetered
on the doorstep, edged
my window. Daylily on her way to dust
divined my heart while you were
madly razoring her stem. None of us
transfigured. I walked through myself, holding
with tenderness her wilted headdress.

VIII.

In the Beautiful Static of Winter

Was sex solely skin and blood, or was it
the bulb you pulled from its heat?
Was it mock-dancing
with the wall? Or pounding the earth
with a spoon? Was it the brutal
ironic dark? A dry call?

    Was it two hands pressed against
another's chest as though to burn through the borders,
or to shield it from itself, its hapless
openness—dear god.

The figures, the figures are
towing their shadows down
the streets, into parking lots
and under a tree.
      Knives and milkweed, stars, stars
all carrying their shadows.

     You tow your shadow. And I mine,
      into a quiet room,
                     into an unforeseen certainty of love.
The shadows are obedient
though we ask nothing of them.

     No! it is the shadows that are towing us —.

In my time before you, I shouted
at walls. I worked with a strange attention
to silence and hid behind partitions,
alone with the wind, transparent and thick,
the high, hounded sound of a body hurt
that cries in the woods so
openly the trees dissolve.

     There is a way the body weds memory—
a marriage like that of a planet to light. My time before you
was light wed to light, sheer and ardent, holy
annihilation.

There are only so many petals
in this room. Freckled ear of tigerlily
I will leave on the table, a few flaps
from the punch-eyed susan strewn
over the carpet, choked purple hyacinth bells
I will slip into an envelope and mail,
some threads from queen anne
for the empty bed, unmade since you
      were a body there. By day's end,
      all petals will be spread—useless
      beauties that I love, every
      bloom you swerved past I will touch.

go where the ghost of the picnic is   grazed
by each other's light we lay   accumulating
memory   there was no rain   the urn
of the throat opened to its ash   blood-
faced berries awoke in our hands   a mallard
gleamed the lake   protecting
what had sunk   the sun-
dials dialed the dark   it answered
and then night lifted us
carrying what was ravaged

In the beautiful static of winter:

somewhere, in that flood
from my body, curled

possibly a she. Limb-buds,
the beginning of a face:

a daughter—lost in water
—quick-ripped aster

spawning
petal-bits, specks half-

floating—.
Nothing doing—.

In winter, I sew my belt
with frozen thistles—

I parse pennies
weightier than she was.

Losses accumulate like pollen—
there's one and it's deadly and beautiful and then the sky
is flowering with ghosts.

   When the body drifts off, there is no voice
to draw it back. Its name lost, its places float
anonymous. Rib of sun, lung of cloud...

Tend to the dead lark
I've hidden in the leaves
from my child
                        This time I'll strap it to my eave
This time wedge it in my mouth   This time
taste its wet feathers   fringe and quill   taste
the intricate bone-work that kept it low and safe between trees
taste the threads of its weave
the faint stitch of blood
taste till the mouth grows blind
to all but its raw signal
                        Let the doors swing open—
                        let the flies descend.

The child and the man are sitting in the same shaft
of light, pointing through a window into the trees.
Son. Husband.

    I am swallowing and swallowing and trying
to keep breathing, however unsteadily. Even in this room
with them, the low warning horns, *alarum alarum*, and I
dissolve....

      Imagine abstaining from that, imagine letting the dark
have its life

     only at night...imagine sleeping inside its brittle cup.
Dear child, Dear man

     what are you seeing? Show me

     the slightest branch, unfiltered—

     the one smelling of moss and rain

for me to press my cheek against.

Kites and cries
loosed from their strings
        in the ongoing sun, flitter of memory, wind
doing what wind does. Everything's
        in upheaval—birds—trees—
        the flashing
ocean that could pull us down in an instant,
currents—as we surface—
        racing beneath us.

The newts shimmy up from the ground, surround
the house with their comical legs and orange embryonic
    translucency, circle the wet stones and slick roots
that reared up decades ago seeming
    furious but getting nowhere. And I am circling after
my orange heart-slips, desiring each one visible, dark-eyed and happy
    in the damp periphery, distant from the forest lumberers gouged
to a butchery of stumps, rot-in-the-danglers, blackout of moss.

    I can almost hold the gaze of the sun lifting high above
the gleaming blood of its pieces.

By scorch or drought or scourging rain
                the peony's white mouth fractured
                                yellowish-brown, the petals frantic
seeming to crawl out of themselves

                                I'm not doing anything but
                                  watching

              myself lop the bloom off
                        straight from the stem
pour gallons of sugar water
                   into its slack mouth

              I am a mother now
regarding the damage   sniffing for new growth   for anything
          sweet or retrievable

I'll later press the petals in a book

When our son knew only sounds, how beautiful
they felt in the mouth, how beautiful our mouths
were in making them, making him laugh or
start, even when you lay beneath a sheet—deflated
as if you'd just fallen there into the bed—
bewildered parachute—cords & wires
loosely snagged to your chest & mouth—while we watched
the nurses' hands all over you, pushing tubes
into your skin, your damaged blood
hidden, but *saved, saved*—

we were glad his heart was too new
to be troubled by this or by the sirens, monitors, the staggering
signals: flash & bleat & bright. We were
glad he played in your wires & sheet. Glad he did
not look at you too silently.

Language will be his some day, will dim
that room & jar him & when we tell our son
of her, will our throats go bare,
will he look at us, tremulous, mouthing
those mouthings no language
can fill—what no word is burn
or bloom enough to say. Will sounds come to him
in irrevocable ways. Or will he disregard our
breath & hers. As many do. As I have done.

I'm walking through petals beside
a child waving a stick
that looks like a wolf. He's not afraid.
He's singing about garbage men
who lug swollen bags away. He's singing
about knives, how we shouldn't
hold them till we're old. Why
even then?
      There is a space
between him and me—a space,
        not a chasm—
        not too wide for our crossing—.

The feathers are auburn, ruby-flecked
and the eyes dark gold. It is a quiet owl
and it watches me watching it. It watches the small
family in the deepening dusk. It watches the house,
the dragged stick, the broken flower. The empty
chair. When I move toward the tree,
it swivels its head. It is a signal—
wanting me to know that it has never left, will never
leave—not when I step into other rooms, not
when I edge closer, not even when it vanishes.

acknowledgments

Grateful acknowledgment is made to the editors of journals and anthologies in which some of these poems appeared, sometimes in earlier versions or with different titles:

Adanna Literary Journal, A Face to Meet the Faces: An Anthology of Contemporary Persona Poetry, 5 A.M., Blackbird, The Cortland Review, Crazyhorse, The Feminist Wire, Handsome, Interim, The Massachusetts Review, Packingtown Review, Pleiades, Ploughshares, Post Road Magazine, VERSE, Verse Daily, VOLT.

Many thanks to my beloved and indefatigable readers who helped to midwife this book: Catherine Barnett, Chris Forhan, Jacqueline Oliva, Dana Roeser. Gratitude to Dr. Kathleen Young for encouraging me to speak. And to Linda Ferreira, who helped me go there and return intact. I feel intense appreciation and admiration for my students who bravely open their hearts and help me to do the same. For E. especially.

Love and thanks to my mother and father and my Grandmother Lynch for being paragons of grit, my most meaningful inheritance — and to my brothers, for your goodness.

Sons Milo and Oliver: your beautiful, kind hearts, your spectacular minds, stories, drawings, puns, paintings, songs, and dancing are sustenance and joy for me.

Steadfast husband Chris, my one and only—thank you for your "discerning Eye" and willingness. Your abiding love makes the here and now feel surer, safer.

I am overwhelmingly grateful to Carey Salerno for her editorial expertise and warm affirmation and extraordinary care for this book. Thanks to Alyssa Neptune, for such good cheer and consistent help. And to all the AJB folk for their commitment to imagination, creativity, vision, and voice.

Without the generous gift of time and space that the Corporation of Yaddo and The MacDowell Colony gave me, these poems would have remained dormant.

I dedicate this book also to my dearmost gruff-hearted SLC don and first-ever poetry teacher—Tom Lux (1946-2017)—who first sang Roethke to me, whose guidance and infinitely generous and forthright spirit I miss, without whom I might have floated farther away —.

Dear Cook Steve A. from 4 Winds: You saw my face. You knew.

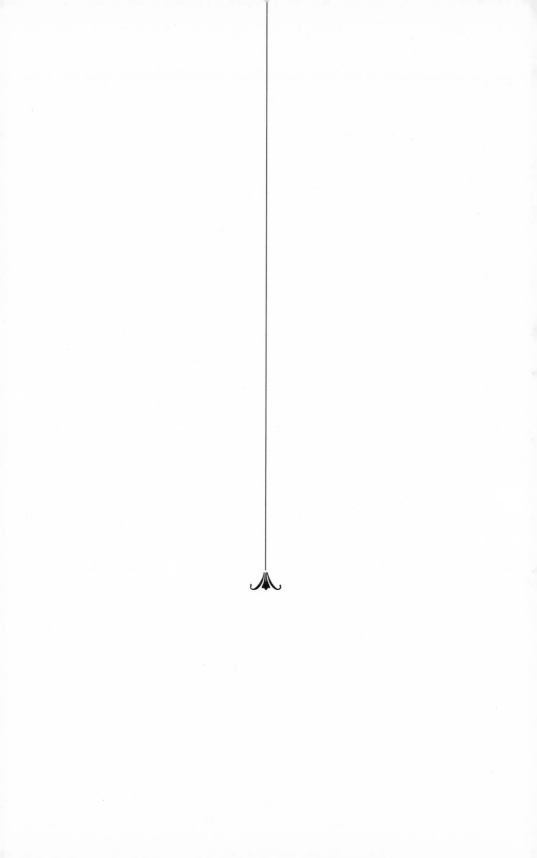

Book Benefactors

Alice James Books wishes to thank the following individuals
who generously contributed toward the publication of
Daylily Called It a Dangerous Moment:

Christopher Forhan
David & Margarete Harvey
Jane Mead
Judith & Glenn Rock

For more information about AJB's book benefactor program,
contact us via phone or email, or visit alicejamesbooks.org
to see a list of forthcoming titles.

Recent Titles from Alice James Books

Alice James Books has been publishing poetry since 1973. The press was founded in Boston, Massachusetts as a cooperative wherein authors performed the day-to-day undertakings of the press. This collaborative element remains viable even today, as authors who publish with the press are also invited to become members of the editorial board and participate in editorial decisions at the press. The editorial board selects manuscripts for publication via the press's annual, national competition, the Alice James Award. Alice James Books seeks to support women writers and was named for Alice James, sister to William and Henry, whose extraordinary gift for writing went unrecognized during her lifetime.

Designed by Pamela A. Consolazio
LITTLE FROG DESIGNS

Printed by McNaughton & Gunn